WATER'S CHILDREN

Written by **Angèle Delaunois**

Illustrated by **Gérard Frischeteau**

Translated by **Erin Woods**

First published in Canada and the United States in 2017
Text copyright © 2017 Angèle Delaunois
Illustration copyright © 2017 Gérard Frischeteau
This edition copyright © 2017 Pajama Press Inc.
Translated from the French by Erin Woods
Originally published in French by éditions de l'Isatis

10 9 8 7 6 5 4 3 2 1

 Canada Council   Conseil des arts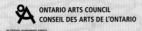
for the Arts   du Canada

The publisher gratefully acknowledges the support of the Canada Council for the Arts and the
Ontario Arts Council for its publishing program. We acknowledge the financial support of the
Government of Canada through the Canada Book Fund (CBF) for our publishing activities.

Library and Archives Canada Cataloguing in Publication

Delaunois, Angèle
[Enfants de l'eau. English]
    Water's children / written by Angèle Delaunois ; illustrated
by Gérard Frischeteau ; translated by Erin Woods.
Translation of: Les enfants de l'eau.
ISBN 978-1-77278-015-4 (hardback)
    1. Water--Juvenile literature. I. Frischeteau, Gérard, 1943-,
illustrator II. Title. III. Title: Enfants de l'eau. English
GB662.3.D4413 2017   j553.7   C2016-906615-0

Publisher Cataloging-in-Publication Data (U.S.)

Names: Delaunois, Angèle, author. | Frischeteau, Gérard, 1943-, illustrator. | Woods, Erin, translator.
Title: Water's Children / written by Angèle Delaunois ; illustrated by Gérard Frischeteau ; translated by Erin Woods.
Description: Toronto, Ontario Canada : Pajama Press, 2016. | Originally published in French as Les
enfants de l'eau. | Summary: "Twelve children from around the world describe how water appears
in their environment, and what it means to them. Their differing experiences are united by the
phrase "water is life," translated into each of their languages"— Provided by publisher.
Identifiers: ISBN 978-1-77278-015-4 (hardcover)
Subjects: LCSH: Water – Juvenile literature. | Water-supply – Juvenile literature. | BISAC: JUVENILE
NONFICTION / Science & Nature / Earth Sciences / Water.
Classification: LCC GB662.3D453 |DDC 551.48 – dc23

Manufactured by Qualibre Inc./Printplus Limited
Printed in China

Pajama Press Inc.
181 Carlaw Ave. Suite 207 Toronto, Ontario Canada, M4M 2S1

Distributed in Canada by UTP Distribution
5201 Dufferin Street Toronto, Ontario Canada, M3H 5T8

Distributed in the U.S. by Ingram Publisher Services
1 Ingram Blvd. La Vergne, TN 37086, USA

TO THE CHILDREN of water who inspire and delight us: Amélia, Audrey, Aurélie, Aurélien, Berthine, Carla, Charlotte, Clovis, Eléa, Florine, Hugo, Joanne, Jules, Justine, Kassandre, Lou, Maya, Maxence, Mélusine, Ophélie, Pauline, Pierre, Quentin, Rose, Thomas, Tristan, and Zoé.

LOOK FOR WATERMARKS throughout the book to learn how "Water is Life" is said in languages around the world. Turn to the last page for a guide to the regions featured.

CHILD OF HERE, child of there, child of water... tell me about the water you see, the water you drink, the water that bathes you.

For me, water is everywhere:
the tap that I turn on without thinking,
the bathtub full of bubbles,
the sprinkler that greens the grass,
the lake that summons us for vacation fun.

For me, water is a burst of laughter.

L'eau c'est la vie

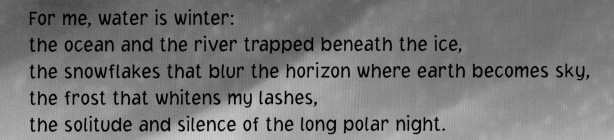

For me, water is winter:
the ocean and the river trapped beneath the ice,
the snowflakes that blur the horizon where earth becomes sky,
the frost that whitens my lashes,
the solitude and silence of the long polar night.

For me, water is a perfect crystal of snow.

For me, water is the dam:
the vast lake that swells in the rain,
the flooding of my ancestors' village,
the old church bell silenced for the sake of new power,
the reservoir that holds the energy to light up distant cities.

For me, water is the night that blazes like day.

For me, water is the ocean:
the gray waves that break on the sand,
the damp air where the gulls soar,
the boat that carries my father into the horizon,
the hold heavy with fish when he returns to port.

For me, water is a sea star.

ВОДА-ЭТО ЖИЗНЬ

For me, water is springtime:
the showers that wash the gray roofs of my town,
the asphalt shining in the streetlights,
the rainbow of umbrellas that bloom on the sidewalk,
the cheerful splash of the fountain.

For me, water is an opening flower.

Wasser ist Leben

For me, water is the immense forest:
the air heavy with rain,
the ancient trees rooted beneath the tide,
the swish of my canoe between the green grasses,
the symphony of birds in the tangle of branches.

For me, water is the breath of the river.

A água é a vida

El agua es la vida

For me, water is the mountain:
the steep paths that lose themselves in mist,
the rainbow where the waterfall meets the sun,
my village snuggled around its well,
the icy stream that waters our gardens.

For me, water is a basket of vegetables.

For me, water is the rice paddy:
the sparkling grid of flooded fields,
the green islets full of young shoots,
my mother and my father planting out the seedlings,
the children and the ducks wading in the mud.

For me, water is a bowl of rice.

水是生命的泉源

For me, water is a long history:
the land my grandfather reclaimed from the desert,
the snaking hose that drips and drips,
the dunes turned into gardens,
the leaves murmuring in old fruit trees.

For me, water is the juice of an orange.

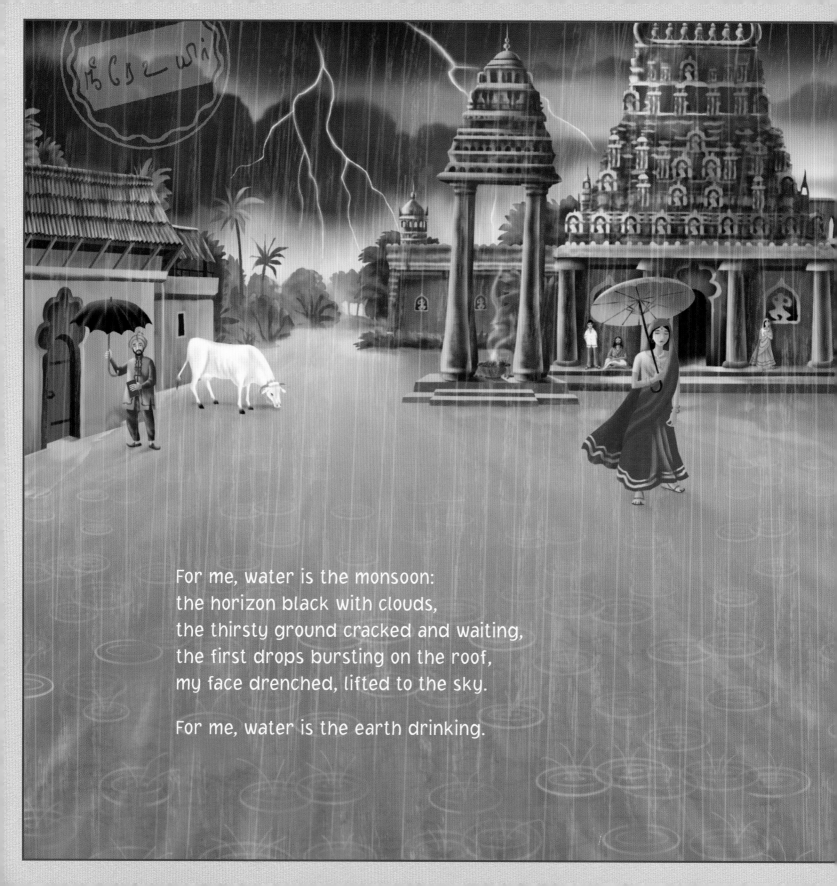

For me, water is the monsoon:
the horizon black with clouds,
the thirsty ground cracked and waiting,
the first drops bursting on the roof,
my face drenched, lifted to the sky.

For me, water is the earth drinking.

For me, water is patience:
silent steps on the fine sand,
the full canteens more precious than gold,
my family's tents under a thousand stars,
the oasis in the distance like a promised land.

For me, water is a cup of mint tea.

For me, water is a miracle:
my abandoned village roasting in the sun,
the endless walk on burning paths,
the shade of the tent where we can sleep at last,
the tank truck that keeps us alive.

For me, water is an outstretched hand.

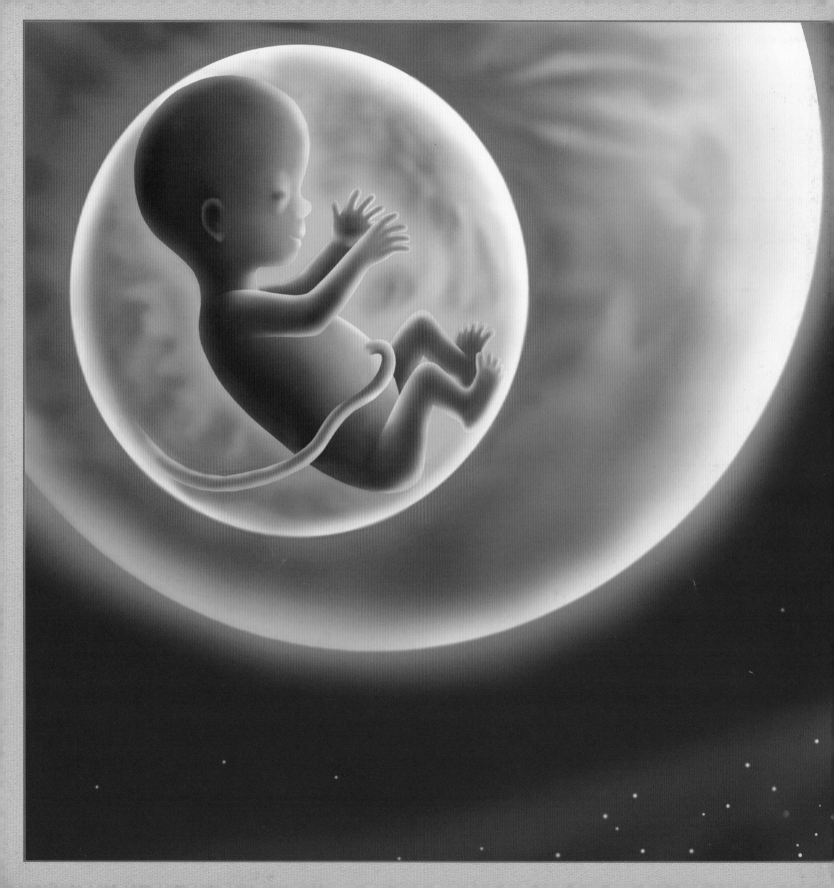

And you, child of the future, child not yet born,
tell me about the water that you see, the water that
surrounds you, the water that bathes you.

For me, water is the song of my mother:
the ocean of her belly where I am transforming myself,
the umbilical cord that helps me to grow.
In this warm bubble, I am a child of water.
I will always be a child of water.

For me, for all of us, water is a matter of life.

Water is life

Our sincere thanks to the following people who translated "Water is life" into different languages:

The burst of laughter (Quebec)
Translation into French: Angèle Delaunois

The crystal of snow (Nunavut)
Translation into Innuktitut: Jacques Pasquet and Harriet Kulutak

The night that blazes like day (Spain)
Translation into Catalan: Gemma Garcia

The sea star (Russia)
Translation into Russian: Daniel Zékina

The opening flower (Germany)
Translation into German: Christel Heitmann

The breath of the river (Brazil)
Translation into Portuguese: Gloria Mamede

The basket of vegetables (Peru/Bolivia)
Translation into Spanish: Dynah Psyché and Laurent Chabin

The bowl of rice (China)
Translation into Chinese: Mei-Kuei Feu

The juice of an orange (Israel)
Translation into Hebrew: Michaël Israël

The earth drinking (India)
Translation into Tamil: Martine Quentric-Séguy and David Annoussany

The cup of mint tea (Morocco)
Translation into Arabic: Hassam El Hadi

The outstretched hand (Mauritania)
Translation into Wolof: Mamadou Dimé